GW00707871

Forward To The Right

A Play of Joan of Arc

Lily Ann Green

Samuel French – London
New York – Sydney – Toronto – Hollywood

FORWARD TO THE RIGHT

First performed at the Ontario One-Act Play Festival in 1981, with the following cast:

The Guard   Ian Wright
The Prisoner   Siri Barrett-Leonard

Directed by David Antscherl

It was subsequently performed at the Cafe Upstairs, London in February 1985, with Martyn Hainstock and Hilary Austin

The action of the play takes place in a jail cell of a castle in Rouen, France

Time—fifteenth Century

FORWARD TO THE RIGHT*

SCENE 1

A jail cell of a castle in Rouen, France. Early in the fifteenth century

The set consists of a cell, distinguishable in whatever way the company sees fit. There is a small stool and a bucket. A small window should be established on one of the four walls, either real or imaginary

As the CURTAIN *rises the stage is dimly lit. The sound of keys jangling and doors opening and closing are heard off*

A rough, middle-aged English soldier enters, he is carrying a cloak, a small satchel, keys and shackles. He wears a well-worn tunic and carries a dagger in his belt

Guard Christ it's dark down here (*He comes into the light*) That's better. Now I can see what the hell I'm doing. (*He sets his things down by the stool*) Jesus, I could almost think I was back home, it's so bloody damp down here. Well not much longer now. (*He takes a look round*) The "frogs" must have learned to build jails from us. Not even her devil's magic will get her out of here. Then we can get this war back on fair terms and we can all go home. (*He sits down, rummaging in his satchel and pulls out a flask*) This job ought to be good for a few rounds at the pub when it's all over. (*He takes a drink*) Shouldn't be too hard keeping an eye on the little lady either. Maybe even a might pleasing.

The Guard begins to take another drink but is interrupted by the sound of doors opening and footsteps approaching

Damn. They're early with her. (*He hastily hides the flask and tidies himself up*) Well, let's to her, John.

---

*N.B. Paragraph 3 on page ii of this Acting Edition regarding photocopying and video-recording should be carefully read.

The Guard exits and returns shortly, roughly pulling the Prisoner in after him and throws her to the floor. She is about nineteen, with straggling, shoulder-length hair, wearing what have been plain, but upper-class, gentleman's clothes. Her hands are chained together and she is tired and weak

Come on you, get up. (*He kicks her*) I said get up.

She moves slightly and he kicks her again

Come on, hurry it up.

She finally struggles to her feet and the Guard proceeds to shackle her ankles

There. Now you won't be jumping out any more windows like you tried doing at Bore-rev-war. (*Beaurevoir—but he pronounces it very badly*) And I won't be standing for any of your nonsense, do you hear? I've heard the stories they've been telling about you. Talking to yourself, going into trances and putting curses on people. Well I ain't going to put up with any of it. Understand? None of your devil's tricks are going to work on me. (*Eyeing her and taunting*) Look at you. They say all the top fellows in your army have been fighting over you. That you must be some sort of beauty. Huh! You're just a scrap of a girl. I can see how you'd be mistaken for a boy all right, but why grown men'd be fighting over you. Unless you used some of your magic on them. Did you do that? Did the holy little "virgin" use magic to get men to fight over her favours? Did she? Did you do that?

Prisoner It is not true.

Guard Oh, so you do understand English, eh? And speak it.

Prisoner I learned a tiny part of your language from the soldiers.

Guard Huh. By witchcraft you mean.

Prisoner I AM NOT A WITCH! Mother of God, give me patience. I am not a witch.

Guard Temper. Temper. The "virgin" who talks to God has a mean little temper so she has.

Prisoner I am sorry.

Guard You're what?

Prisoner I am sorry. For my temper. (*Under her breath*) Mon Dieu, pardonne-moi. Il faut que j'apprenne à me taire. [My dear God forgive me. I have yet to learn to hold my tongue]

Guard What did you just say?

Prisoner I ask my God's forgiveness.

Guard Yeh. I think I got that much. What was the rest of it?

Prisoner I said I must learn to . . . (*She gropes for the correct word*) mind my words.

Guard Oh. Well this might still be France, but this is an English fort now, and you're in an English jail. So you're to speak English while you're here with me. You understand?

She nods

Good. (*He sits down, pulls some food out of the satchel and starts eating, using his dagger*) You could be saying anything, right in front of me and I wouldn't even know it.

There is a long moment of silence while the Guard eats and the Prisoner slowly walks around the cell. The only sounds are from the Guard's knife and the clatter of the Prisoner's shackles

Would you sit down for Christ's sake! Or at least stay still for a bloody minute. You're making enough noise to wake the dead.

The Prisoner stops and turns to him, watching him eat. It has been a long time since she has even seen "real" food, she does not realize she is staring or that this is making the Guard nervous

Will you sit down?

The Prisoner sits but continues watching him

Why don't you say something for Christ's sake?

Prisoner What do you wish me to say?

Guard I don't know! Something. Anything, damn it.

Prisoner (*after a pause, examining her ankle chains*) Am I considered so dangerous that I must be chained so thoroughly?

Guard You almost escaped once.

Prisoner But my illness was my punishment. I have promised I will not try again.

Guard (*laughing*) You promise? That's a laugh that is. As if anyone would believe a promise from a prisoner, especially a French one. And a witch.

Prisoner I am not a witch and anyone who believes I am is a sinner in the eyes of my Father God, and will have to answer to Him.

Guard You listen here. Don't you go throwing any of your curses around me.

Prisoner It is not a curse. It says in the Bible, "whosoever . . . "

Guard (*interrupting*) I wouldn't know. I haven't read the Bible lately.

Prisoner Neither have I. But I have had verses read to me since I was a child. I never learned to read. (*She pauses*) Did no one ever read the Bible to you?

Guard I don't remember.

Prisoner I could recite . . .

Guard Will you shut up for God's sake!

Prisoner But you wished me to speak to you.

Guard Well, I changed my mind.

Doors opening and footsteps are heard offstage

That'll be your dinner. (*He starts to exit then stops and looks at her suspiciously*) I don't suppose you can disappear in two seconds?

Prisoner (*in French*) Pardon?

Guard Just don't fly away.

The Prisoner does not understand

No. (*He shakes his head*) Fly. (*He flaps his arms*) Away. (*He mimes "away"*)

The Guard, realizing he has made a slight fool of himself, exits hastily and returns very quickly carrying a tin plate of unappetizing mush. He slides it along the floor to her

There you go. Enjoy.

The Prisoner makes no move towards the plate

Well, what's the matter? You haven't eaten in at least a day, you must be starving.

There is a pause

Well go on! It's not going to get better looking with age.

There is a pause

Well, if you don't like it, why don't you change it into a venison pie with all the trimmings?

Prisoner I am not hungry, thank you.

Guard You aren't going to go making yourself ill while you're my "responsibility". So you just go ahead and eat. They want you good and healthy for trial.

Prisoner (*pulling the plate closer for inspection*) What is it?
Guard (*returning to his own meal*) Bread and milk.
Prisoner Oh, du pain et du lait.
Guard Do pen eh what?
Prisoner (*slowly*) Du pain et du lait.
Guard You mean do pain eh ... whatever you said, is that? (*He points to her meal*)
Prisoner Oui. Bread and milk.
Guard Yes.
Prisoner On the boat I had only bread and water.
Guard Well there, you see? Things are looking up ain't they? (*He pulls an apple out of his satchel and takes a few bites then studies it*) Apple. What do you call it?

The Prisoner does not understand

(*Holding the apple up*) What is this?
Prisoner La pomme.
Guard (*trying*) La pomme.
Prisoner (*pleased*) Yes.
Guard Huh. La pomme (*He grunts, bites the apple and points to her plate*) Eat. (*He continues eating*)
Prisoner (*pushing the plate from her*) They think all of this, the chains, the lack of food, that all of it will make me weak and give in. But they are wrong. It can only strengthen me. You will see.

They watch each other a moment, then the Prisoner stands and walks to the bucket. The Guard resumes his meal

It is not filled.
Guard What?
Prisoner The ... Le seau. (*She points to the bucket*) It is not filled.
Guard (*pointing*) That? It's a bucket. Buck-et. And it ain't supposed to be filled. It's. ... (*He suddenly doesn't know how to explain*) You're supposed to ... Well what the hell did you do on the ship for Christ's sake?

After much thought she slowly realizes what he means

Prisoner On the boat it had a ... un covercle, a ... cover, so that it would not smell. (*Then as an afterthought*) And I was alone.
Guard I'll close my eyes.

The Prisoner is morally shocked

Then I'll ... Damn it to hell, then you tell me when and I'll ... Christ! ... I'll go into the corridor. But the minute somebody's coming I'm back in.

Prisoner Thank you.

Guard Don't thank me, damn it. (*He picks a stick up off the floor and starts whittling*)

There is a pause

Prisoner (*staring up at the window*) Why would one make a window where there is nothing to see but stone wall?

Guard It's to give you air.

Prisoner Oh.

The Guard continues whittling, the Prisoner twists around, leaning eventually forward, and to the right, looking out of the window

I found some sky!

The Guard, startled, jumps and cuts his finger

Guard Jesus Christ! You made me cut my bleeding finger for Christ's sake.

Prisoner I'm sorry. Is it bad?

Guard I'll live.

Prisoner Should you not clean it? Or wrap it?

Guard It'll be all right.

Prisoner You are sure?

Guard Yes, I am.

Prisoner Oh. Bon. Good. I did not mean to frighten you. I was just so pleased to see something, not wall. It helps me if I can see something that God has made. Now I know that every morning if I sit below this window and tilt my head forward and to the right just a tiny amount, I can see that little patch of sky. And then I will be able to go on with the day. At Beaurevoir I had to stand on the bed, on my toes to look out of the window. But then I could see a meadow full of sheep and trees. On the boat I could see nothing, but I could hear the waves hitting the walls. I had never dreamt of so much water at once in my whole life before that. It was ... très belle.

Guard I get sea sick.

Prisoner As did I. But still it was très belle. (*She watches him whittle*) What are you making?

Guard Nothing.

Prisoner Then why do it?

Guard Passes time.

Prisoner But why just pass time and not enjoy every bit of it that God has given to you? (*She watches him a while longer*) You don't trust me.

Guard (*sarcastically*) Now why would you think that? Just because you're French and I'm English and you're a prisoner and I'm guarding you, now why wouldn't I trust you?

Prisoner It is more than that. It is all these stories about my being a witch. You think I will disappear or put some curse on you. You even think I used witchcraft to make you cut your finger. Do you not? It was not so.

Guard And how do I know that eh? Maybe you did it to ... to punish me ... for ... for swearing at you.

Prisoner All soldiers swear. My comrades always swore in front of me. They do not understand what they swear against and do not care. It does not offend me.

Guard Then it could be something else. For locking you up.

Prisoner You were ordered to do that.

The Guard continues whittling

(*To herself*) Holy Saint Catherine, why does no one believe me now? Charles did. He trusted me. (*To the Guard*) If I were a witch, could I not unlock these chains, that door? Maybe I could vanish. But I have not. Does that not prove to you I am no witch?

Guard No. You just have some reason for staying around. Maybe the French are just pretending to hate you and you're spying on us. Then you'll get all sorts of information and disappear just before they're to burn you.

Prisoner Burn me.

Guard That's the punishment for heresy and witchcraft. You're charged with both. Shame they can't burn you twice.

Prisoner Have the Bishops decided if I may take communion?

Guard Aye. You can't.

Prisoner May I attend mass?

Guard No.

Prisoner Will my rosary be returned to me?

Guard Look. The way I understand it is this. Until you decide to wear women's clothing and quit claiming to talk to angels, you can't have any of those things.

Prisoner I do not understand any of this. I did nothing to them. Am I to be punished for speaking the truth and doing God's will? What do they want from me?

Guard Blood.

Prisoner What?

Guard Blood. The French want you for losing Paris. The priests want you for riling the peasants and us English want you for taking Orleans the way you did . . .

Prisoner What we did at Orléans was no worse than what the English did at Paris, or any other battle.

Guard But we don't kill people in God's name, now do we?

Prisoner No. You do it in your English King's name and call it righteous. (*She goes to the window and prays quietly to herself*) Oh dearest God, give me strength.

The Guard stops whittling but is almost afraid to turn around

I know it is Your will that I suffer in this way and I accept it. It makes me proud to think that I was thought strong enough to do Your work, but I am frightened Lord. I know that You would let no harm come to me, but still I am tired and frightened. Please God help me I feel so alone.

Guard (*cutting in on her prayer*) Hey! I told you . . . Stop that!

The Prisoner begins to turn to him but then hears something and turns to it. She goes down on her knees and crosses herself

Prisoner Blessed Saint Michael. I had hoped our Lord God would send you to me. I am in such need of the comfort your visits bring. I try to be strong, but it becomes more difficult each day. (*She pauses to listen*) I will do as you say. (*She listens*) Thank you. (*She smiles*) Yes, that is what I needed from you. It sets my heart at ease to hear it. (*She crosses herself and continues in silent prayer*)

Guard (*cutting in on her prayer*) Hey! Stop it! Did you hear me? I said to stop it. Damn it, I told you to stop that.

The Guard grabs her and pulls her head back so that she is looking up at him

I told you I wouldn't be standing for none of this talking to devils didn't I? And I meant it, I did. I'll teach you to cross me.

Prisoner They are not devils, they are angels.

Guard I don't care what you call them. I'm not standing for any of it you hear? I'll teach you to go against me like that you . . . slut . . . devil's whore. (*He straddles her and pins her to the ground*)

Prisoner Holy Saint Catherine help me.

Guard (*slapping her*) Shut up damn you! I'll bet you wouldn't scream so loud for your bleedin' saints if I was one of your high-class French soldiers would you? You bloody little French slut. You think you're too goddamn good for the likes of me don't you, eh? I'll show you a real man. I'm not one of your froggy mincing men.

Prisoner (*calmly and clearly*) May the Lord God forgive you, John Gray.

Guard (*silently and slowly backing away from her*) How did you know my name?

Prisoner I don't know. That's the way it happens. It is as though I hear someone whispering to me, but no one is there.

Guard No. No you ain't going to trick me like that. You heard the others say my name that's all. It's one of your tricks. To make me scared of you. Well it ain't going to work. (*He sits down and picks up his cloak to put it on, but notices a tear*)

Prisoner It was right? The name, John Gray?

Guard Yea. It was right. (*He finds a needle and thread in his satchel and begins a clumsy attempt to thread it*)

Prisoner (*watching with amusement; moving closer*) I have never known a man who could thread a needle. Here, let me.

The Prisoner reaches out for the needle and thread and the Guard gives them to her much to his own surprise, but not hers. She threads the needle easily and holds out her hand

There. Cloak.

The Guard pauses, then gives her the cloak like an obedient child. He is surprised and confused. As the Prisoner settles down to her task, the Lights fade

SCENE 2

The same. Three months later

As the Lights come up we see there is now a lid on the bucket, a pail of drinking water with a tin cup, and a small, dirty scrap of a blanket

The Prisoner and Guard enter. She is very subdued and carries a neatly folded bundle of women's clothing. He carries his satchel

During the following dialogue, she sets down the clothing in a corner and returns to the Guard, who has sat down on his stool. He unlocks her wrist shackles, but she removes them herself, and then unlocks the ankle chains with the keys he tosses to her. He removes a tangle of string from his satchel and begins to occupy himself with untangling it and then trying to make a cat's cradle

Prisoner Shall I tell you?

Guard If you want.

Prisoner They asked about my voices again. Will they never tire of that John? They began of course by asking me how I was feeling and expressing great concern for my health. Bishop Rien, that's the tall, skinny one you imitate so well, he said he hoped they had not tired me too much yesterday, as it was the first full day of court since my illness.

Guard What did you say to all that?

Prisoner I was very nice. I said that I had slept well and I felt much stronger and appreciated their concern for me.

Guard Concern. Huh. That's a laugh that is. You know why they're so "concerned", don't you? If you died here in jail it would only make them look bad. As if you was mistreated or something. (*He pauses*) What then?

Prisoner I told them my Father in Heaven sends me the strength I require. And they asked me how.

Guard What did you tell them this time?

Prisoner The same. That I am not permitted to speak of that yet.

Guard And?

Prisoner They asked me if I meant my angels.

Guard You know you cause all your own troubles? You always say just what they need to condemn you.

Prisoner Am I to lie then, John? (*She pauses*) They asked if they had visited me lately.

Guard And you said?

Prisoner What I always say. They visit me every day.

Guard What did they say to that?

Prisoner They were surprised that my angels would visit me in an English prison. I told them that surely this was where they would visit me more than ever. Then they asked what the voices tell me.

Guard You didn't.

Prisoner I told them what I have told you. The truth. That my voices tell me to be strong and not afraid. That I have nothing to fear because I have done nothing wrong.

Guard They want you dead.

Prisoner I know. But the Holy Mother protects her daughters.

Guard (*softly to himself*) Christ Almighty.

Prisoner I told them my voices said long ago that I would be captured and roughly treated, that I would be hated and threatened. And now they tell me I will be released. And I believe them.

Guard Christ! I don't want to hear this.

Prisoner Bishop Cauchon looked like his head was full of hot steam and would burst. He screamed at me "This is heresy!" I very quietly reminded him that it was only belief in the Lord God and the Holy Virgin.

Guard That's one fellow who won't show you no mercy.

Prisoner I expect none.

Guard What happened then?

The Prisoner goes to the clothing and holds some of it up for the Guard to see

Prisoner They gave me these. I have until morning. If I put them on I may take communion, go to mass, and stay alive.

Guard So you'll do it?

Prisoner What else am I to do John? I do not want to die! But, damn it, they've . . . (*She quickly covers her mouth with her hand when she realizes what she has said*)

Guard (*laughing*) Christ. I hope you didn't use words like that up there.

Prisoner It is not funny. It is only a bad habit which I have been getting from you. If you would mind your tongue——

Guard (*interrupting*) Wait a bloody minute! If you think I'm going to watch what I say so's you don't pick up any new words, you've got another think coming. Why don't you pray for the strength not to let them slip out of your mouth and leave mine out of it? (*He goes back to his string*) So your voices were right? You don't have to die.

Prisoner I suppose . . . Yes. They were right. I don't have to die.

Guard Well, if it's almost over, then I should be getting home soon.

The Prisoner goes to the Guard and joins in the cat's cradle

Though they'll probably find some reason for keeping me here.

Prisoner You miss it? (*She indicates the cat's cradle*) No, under now.

Guard Aye. I like understanding what people are saying to me. (*Referring to the cat's cradle*) Hey, it worked.

The Prisoner wanders over to the pile of clothing

You want me to leave so you can change into those things?

Prisoner Yes please.

The Guard exits

The Prisoner watches the Guard leave and then slowly picks up the clothing as if to put it on. Holding it up to herself she goes to the window

Most sweet Lord, in honour of Your Holy passion, I beseech you, if you love me, to reveal to me what I should answer to these churchmen. I know by whose command I am dressed so, but I do not know whether or not I am to change it now. (*She prays silently for a moment and then turns quickly as though she hears something behind her*) Saint Michael you . . . No! Please don't leave me, I need you. (*She turns back to the window*) Dearest God. Be with me and give me strength so that I may clearly hear your words. (*She kneels and prays a moment longer, then crosses herself and slowly folds the clothing and returns it to the corner*) You may come back in now, John.

The Guard enters

Guard Well, that didn't take you . . . (*He sees that she has not changed into the clothes*) What the hell did you do that for?

Prisoner What?

Guard Your clothes damn it. Why didn't you change them?

Prisoner Because I was not meant to.

Guard Your bloody voices told you that I suppose?

Prisoner Yes.

Guard You realize you've as well as lit the damn fire yourself? This was your last chance.

Prisoner I've prayed about this for a long time John. And I realize now what my fate must be.

Guard You and your bloody prayers. What about your bleedin' voices telling you you're going to be set free. This is their way of doing it I suppose?

Prisoner I realize this is very difficult for you to understand John. I am just beginning to myself. But I realize now that I misunderstood them. My voices. When they told me I would be released they did not mean just from this prison. They meant I would never again have to endure pain or answer question after question. They meant that my soul would be released from this weak body of mine. I don't pretend to know or understand His reasons, but I put myself in His hands.

Guard You mean you're all set to die. To frizzle to death, in front of a crowd of bloodthirsty bastards and it don't bother you?

Prisoner It bothers me. It scares me John. You cannot imagine how frightened I am. But I know that God and my angels will give me the strength I need. (*She pauses*) May He send you strength as well.

Guard Me? Don't bother. It just seems to me that it'd be a hell of a lot easier for everyone if you'd just put on those clothes like they want. Then you could do all the things you've been begging to do for months. And live out a nice long life.

Prisoner Like this!? Living on bread and milk. Breathing stale air? Where the only piece of beauty I have is one tiny patch of sky that I have to crouch and twist to see? No thank you! I'd rather die a horrible death than live such a horrible life.

Guard Well it's your choice. It's not as if it matters to me. As long as I get to go home.

The Prisoner picks up the clothes and takes them to the Guard.

Prisoner You might as well send these back to them. Tell them to give them to some young woman who really needs them.

Guard You realize they won't let you have no sort of ceremony. Not now.

Prisoner I realize it.

The Guard busies himself with some task at his stool while the Prisoner, after a moment's thought, quietly puts a part of the clothing on over her own clothes. The Guard does not notice this

There.

The Guard looks at her

Do you really think that this could make such a difference? Do you actually think this could change everything John?
Guard You look ridiculous.
Prisoner Exactly.

The Guard takes some food out of his satchel while she takes off the women's clothing. He breaks off a piece of food and automatically hands it to her over his shoulder. She takes it just as automatically and the Lights fade as they both eat

SCENE 3

The same

As the Lights come up we see that the bucket's lid, drinking pail, tin cup and blanket are gone

The Guard is alone, huddled in a corner, minus his belt, knife, keys, cloak and satchel. He is wearing the shackles

Guard Well, John my son. You certainly got yourself in a fix this time, didn't you? You've done some stupid things, but this time you outdid yourself. How did you plan to get out of this one eh? Never thought of that, did you? (*He pauses and looks about him, then, focusing on a spot where the prisoner used to sit, he speaks to her*) It's all your doing ain't it? Didn't I risk my neck to be good to you? Shared my meals with you. Talked to you. Explained things to you. And didn't I always slow down when we was walking to the courtrooms so's you could get some fresh air? Mind you, I liked it too. I was stuck down here all day, every day, same as you. But I could've got whipped for it if anyone caught on. But you always said there was no need to worry. As if you knew. As if you really knew. How you got me to do all those things for you, I'll never know. Maybe you was a witch. (*He* *pauses*) No. She just had this way about her. She swore she saw angels. She bloody well talked to them enough. Always down on her knees praying before going to court. And the minute we're back she'd be at it again. (*He pauses*) But now you've done it, haven't you? Fixed me good you have. It wasn't enough you got me to sneak a priest down here to give you last rites this morning. I never did understand all the fuss about that. You'd be going to Heaven with or without it. How could you not? (*He pauses*) Bloody hell John, quit blaming her. You're the fool that did it right in front of everyone. Christ! I must be the laughing stock of His Majesty's Army. They make this big announcement how she's to have no blessing, no cross, no nothing. And you go do what you did. (*He pauses*) But she looked so ... and she reckoned she was doing something important. (*He suddenly looks up and confronts God, above and around him, embarrassed and self-conscious*) She reckoned it was all part of some great plan of Yours! Was it so wrong to let her have something of Yours while she was burning to death for You? Could it have been so wrong? She looked so ... confused. That was it. Confused. As if none of it fitted together and made sense to her. (*Slowly*) And I ain't never heard a scream like that before. And then she looked ... ashamed. And she asks for a cross and I see the Bishop that was running the trial. He just stood there. I swear he was smiling. One priest started to give her his rosary, and that bastard hit him. I wanted to kill him. So I grabbed two sticks and I tied them together with my bit of string and I gives it to her. (*He pauses*) It helped. Or it seemed to. She got quieter. It didn't take long after that. (*He pauses, then laughs*) Helluva way to get yourself shipped home though, ain't it lad? (*He slowly stands up and moves towards the entrance*) Hey! You out there! I know what you want. You want me to say "Yea! Yea, she used witchcraft to make me do all those things." I could even make up some more things and you'd believe me, wouldn't you? Sure you would. You need to. You need to feel better. That maybe you didn't burn a poor little girl to death for nothing. You need to be sure, don't you? Well I won't say it. (*He pauses*) It'd be easy. Real easy. Get me off the hook it would. But I won't. You hear me? I won't. I won't help you rest easy! If a little bit of a girl can stand up to you, then so can I. I won't say it. I did all those things 'cause I wanted to. You hear? Because I wanted to! I wanted to!

He collapses slowly, exhausted, on to the floor, beneath the window. He is quiet and very still for a long time and then slowly he moves, experimenting, into the position we watched the Prisoner twist into in the first scene, to look out of the window, and gradually a small smile appears on his face

Well. What do you know? You can see a bit of sky through there.

BLACK-OUT

FURNITURE AND PROPERTY LIST

LIGHTING PLOT

No practical fitting required

SCENE 1

To open: dim lighting

Cue 1   The **Prisoner** settles down to her task   (Page 9)
The Lights fade

SCENE 2

To open: dim lighting
Cue 2   The **Guard** and the **Prisoner** eat   (Page 14)
The Lights fade

SCENE 3

To open: dim lighting

Cue 3   **Guard** "... a bit of sky through there".   (Page 16)
Black-out

EFFECTS PLOT

MADE AND PRINTED IN GREAT BRITAIN BY
LATIMER TREND & COMPANY LTD, PLYMOUTH
MADE IN ENGLAND